P9-AFD-871

THE SNAKE HUNTER

THE SNAKE HUNTER

Harry Morris

University of Georgia Press, Athens

ACKNOWLEDGMENT

The author and the publisher gratefully acknowledge permission to reprint the following poems which originally appeared in the magazines and books here noted: "A Remembrance of Some American Poets," *College English* (by permission of the National Council of Teachers of English); "In Your Beauty's Orient Deep," *Critical Quarterly;* "The Historie of the World," *The Literary Review;* "In a Field," "And Pays Us But With Age and Dust," and "The Prince and the Tower," *Perspective;* "Central Figure," *Poetry Review;* "Girod Street Cemetery: New Orleans," *The Golden Year: The Poetry Society of America Anthology (1910–1960);* "Pastoral," *Prairie Schooner* (copyright 1959 by the University of Nebraska); "Three-Lined Salamander," *Quartet;* "The Snake Hunter," "Lady Ralegh's Lament," and "I Am Black, But Comely, O Ye Daughters of Jerusalem," *The Sewanee Review* (copyright 1968 by the University of the South); "Here's Fine Revolution, an We Had the Trick to See 't," "The Tower and the Maze," "Noisome Weeds," and "As It Were a Tale," *Southern Poetry Review;* "They Hain't Nothin' Stupider'n a Cow Less'n Hit's a Chicken," *Southern Writing in the Sixties: Poetry* (copyright 1967 by the Louisiana State University Press); "The Thread," *University Review;* "Rapunzel," *Western Humanities Review.*

Library of Congress Catalog Card Number: 70-90560
Standard Book Number: 8203-0243-0

Contents

Preface

Myths told of reptiles are so plentiful they are like one of their own breed. If tail to mouth, they would, like the midgard worm, encircle the earth. These myths remind me of many contemporary practices employed in the name of poetry. So numerous they are that they strangle the art as the serpent would throttle the world.

The myths are ultimately harmless. The person who comes upon a coachwhip snake in the fields will not be chased and thrashed to death, who picks up the beautiful red-bellied mud snake will find no sting in its tail to poison him, who collects the rattle from our awesome diamondback will shake no dust from it to blind him first, then kill him through his eyes.

I am not altogether assured that the falsehoods which pass for poetry will do as little damage. In all creative endeavors, we have passed into a phase where anything a man "can get away with" is sealed as art. In verse, any crudity of language may be termed poetry by the botcher. Unless we can clear up the myths about our craft, I fear that, though some heroes challenge them with the strength that form and tradition give, the monsters in their death throes will vomit their venom and poetry may not survive.

Harry Morris

August 1969
Tallahassee, Florida

For Nancy

FIELD

In a Field

The sky curves over, equally far from land
And foot. Dallying north, a wedge of three
Wild geese, honking spasmodically, dip
And penetrate a canyon rent in clouds,
A gust, contrapuntally, now and then,
Raising or lowering a bird from the line
Of flight. A whirling funnel of wind receives
The universe in loins too small. The Vee
Of the shoulder takes the Vee of the migrants; clouds
Billow and billow in swelling thunderhead
Thrusts at heaven.

                    So much for below.

Twin elbows in the earth bestride twin pools
That mirror everything above. Three ants
Lance swiftly home—a cratered mound; each leaps
Into volcanic warmth, Empedocles
Dying in the erupting womb. The leaves,
Dead and curled, rise on the wind; small puffs of red
And brown and silvered grey play and hold back
And burst in scattered death. The branches of
The hazel, drooping to the ground, entwine
In spreading hair, its roots divining life.

3

Indigo

Modern cartoonists try to teach us men
The devil's flesh is red; but ancient tracts
Still show Old Scratch has not upon his skin
The glow of flames God broiled him in, but black,

The color of his soul and cinder fret.
Evil, too, is like a hard coal mine
Or like an indigo snake. In feeble light
They both seem black; but new-expose a vein

Or scute and both reveal a prism hue.
Black alone contains all shades; and hide
That once wears black upon it comes from the slough,
Not black, but like the indigo—new-shed

And caught in light—a spectrum after rain
Of green and gold and violet, not long
Till dull again in winter discipline,
Yet shed again with every rising spring.

Why Give Goodly Wings to the Peacock?

My peacock clowns it more than treads with pride.
He loafed three years toward plumage and full span.
But still he puffed before he had his train.
He jetted and he strode, spread puny fan
At any creature moving in the yard.

He wooed and courted bantams, ducks, and geese.
He leered at three-day chicks as well as pup
And kitten. He even pranced in hope to tup
A building block left careless on a slope
Of lawn. Now fledged, with pencil-shadowed eyes

In his array, he has a peahen queen.
He jets and struts, shakes all his plumes, performs
His dance, and seems to offer her rare charms
Of feathered glory without end. But his storms
Of lust she spurns, and he must ever preen.

Three-Lined Salamander

Big-eyed, hissless S, I have found you:
Once deep in a frigid pool in a niche of a pitchy
Cave; once mud-snug under a rotten loblolly
Bough; once pressed beneath a rock in a blue

Mountain stream; once clinging up-so-down
To a branch-bank overhang; always cold
And out of sight until I saw, in an old
Poem, you in a line which the prince and clown

Speaks: You lived in the sea-midst when it blazed
And were not drowned and were not burnt or crazed.

Because Robin Forgot the Birds

Where are there livery, hover, and cry?
And what are the field, the forest, and hill?
Without pipit, accentor, and yellowbill?
    With marsh quail
    And boat-tail
    And black rail
    And whip-poor-will.

With tomwalk and scud, jigget and perch,
With dibble and dabble, jug-jug and shrill,
With pipit, accentor, and yellowbill.
    With marsh quail
    And boat-tail
    And black rail
    And whip-poor-will.

Before there were bulldozer, drag-line, and crane,
Trees were unnumbered, bogs stood there still,
With pipit, accentor, and yellowbill.
    With marsh quail
    And boat-tail
    And black rail
    And whip-poor-will.

How Much More Shall Your Heavenly Father

It was a season for birds. Love whirred down
Like waxwings on a stand of myrtle, dove
Among corn, in windy descent, mighty hover,
Landing and cleaving tongues from the sun.

Cold lashed them south, the woods and fields forgot
For lack of food, for unrelenting frost.
The beating wings of such a flaming host
Must drive the heart; the heart so fledged will not

Beat off the host. Unutterable numbers of dove
In the hunter-banished field will strip the stalks,
The later famine leave but coat and sticks;
But even the thieving crow will be fed by love.

For, Indeed, There Is No Goodness in the Worm
—To my son

The gaily banded snake you found,
Though he wear motley—yellow, red,
Yellow, black—is not a clown
But that which goes with clownish blood.
Although you love the worm, "the worm's
An odd worm." He cannot love you;
And you must be content, since God's
Own love worked no responding glow.
One revel-suited worm, more bright
By far than red and yellow, could
Not love his loving Lord. For that
He now is black. And though I bid
You "joy o' the worm," I trust you mind,
Dear Chris, "that the worm will do his kind."

9

They Hain't Nothin' Stupider'n a Cow
Less'n Hit's a Chicken

I once had a cow named Isabella who fell
In love with my tractor. She came under the spill
Of the moon one night it was full and those sixty-inch
    wheels
Raised a broad and potent hump and planted heels

Firm for the push. I couldn't plow but what
She'd follow; and, unlike any other stock,
A turn that brought me down a furrow right
Road for her skeered her not a bushel bait.

I almost plowed her good those times and whiles
She showed her thing to me and twitched her tail.
I found her dead one night I couldn't sleep
(The moon full), near the tractor all aheap.

Almanac

When I was seven, I had a mallard hide
Her eggs in a hollow pecan tree. She was trod
Early and laid early in February.
I put my head in the hole one day to number
The clutch when a flicker thrummed the trunk.

"Thunder!"

I cried and wept for the delicate pinks I set
Early, up early, early doomed, wept
With poulter-ploughman's wisdom that warns of winter
Malice to early husbandry, wept for thunder
In February that tokens an April frost.

Yellow hammer, yellow hammer ringed
My tree and all my early springtime dinged.

II

When I was twelve behind an oak I came
Upon a coachwhip snake. I could not run.
It was so warm for February, I knew
The snake was active-warm. He'd chase and flail
Me dead. Instead he only drummed his tail
Upon the leaves, a noise like thunder in
My ears, and "Thunder!" I cried and wept again
The tender, naked young, born early, in winter
Out early, early ended; wept for thunder
In February that tokens an April frost.

Coachwhip snake, coachwhip snake lashed
Dead leaves and all my early springtime smashed.

Here's Fine Revolution, an We Had
the Trick to See 't

The pond was nearly dry the year I took
This place; and once, before I came, it sloped
Only to dust. I think a predecessor
Stocked it next, but I am no confessor
To the mysteries of life; yet I have groped
For bass in some peculiar ponds to hook

A bluegill there. Sun-dwindled and unfished pools
May have a lot of fish, but they will all
Be small: the food too scarce, the waters strait.
This year the pond has spread—the rain so great—
It benefits my neighbor too. By fall
The older bass had got so large, new schools

Were merely food. Now bass control the rushes.
They swallow spawn and minnow, tadpole, newt,
And salamander; wide-mouthed, swift, they take
The young of snapping turtle, gator, and snake.
There's too much water now. We need an acute
Dry season, ye gods, and little fishes.

Tortoises and Diamondbacks

Gophers are good burrowers, fixed with plain
Implements and instincts for delving down.
Under the light of the summer world, they mine
Only their own shell, but in winter's moon,
In tedious wet, in gray, in cold, they shun

The upper planes, enearthing for one-third
Or so within the holes sometimes as long
As thirty feet they cannily provide
Against the chilling times. When hunters bring
Their gopher hooks to drag one out, the prong

Must deftly strike or he will further crawl
Another terrace deeper in his pit.
Diamondbacks lack tools for digging, will
At times house with a gopher, six, seven, eight
To the hole. The gopher must behave; he cannot fight.

It Was Never Meant to Be Easy

Christopher Ridge offers the fairest view
In Clay county. It tops a wooded hill
In the southern Smokies, live with whippoorwill
To the crab apple at the peak, bright with dew.

The climb was hard for me. I've had a fall
From a fruit tree in my flatland garden plot.
Still, no good thing was ever easily got.
But now I may have lost the ridge for all

Time. The owner's closed the surrounding land.
All I can see is the tree against the sky.
Unless the man gives me an easement, I
Believe I'll lose the final climb I planned.

The Snake Hunter

Emily knew the icy tines that rake
Along a vagrant frame at the sight of a snake.
But I know a man who hunts for harmless breeds
In a place where all the deadly sorrow speeds

Of poison in eight fangs, a place where four
Rivers, wide apart at their source, become
Two and issue at a sandy shore.
Magnolia, footed in fluvial slime and scum,

Overhang the St. Marks, and sweet gum crowd
To waters of the Wacissa. Dogwood, loud
In their fall of blossom, eloquently tongue
The Aucilla, and cypress, dead and down among

The prostrate years of half a century
Ago, lie athwart the Wakulla, rim-
Wood still unrotted by the salt-near sea.
He finds upon a divining sun-drenched limb

An emerald climbing snake and, up the bank,
Black racers. In the wooded flats and rank
Mulch he pinions indigos and queens,
Bright scarlet kings and lusterless keeled greens.

He preys on preyers: rat snakes, chicken, corn,
And oak snakes. His musty croker sack reveals
On opening God's covenant, forsworn
In rainbow snakes caught under his bruising heels.

Down every wooded slope and in each field,
Each briar-studded brake, a choice is sealed
Of right or left, straight road, around some bole:
Lift rocks, roll logs, or probe some probable hole.

I do not see how he can fail the lair,
The great live oak, the rattler grinning there.

CHAMBER

Rapunzel

How could he think to find her always there?
Those widened eyes and soft lips—motionless—
Her love, the golden ladder of her hair
Unwound each day to raise to paradise
A witch deranged by so much loveliness.
What could have saved him from that sacrifice?

Unsound, he leaped to bleeding thorns of love
Who only wished to climb a sun-washed skein
Of hair, ate berries brought him by a dove,
And wandered in the wildness of a dream,
At roots of blackened trees still crying everywhere,
"Rapunzel, Rapunzel, let down your hair."

Somehow in all that darkness he unlocked her sighs,
Lamenting something lost in bitter flashes;
She wept her tears upon his clotted lashes,
And he saw again. His fingers questioned strands
Of violated hair; his silvered eyes
Wept blood-red crystals on his bloodless hands.

I Raise a Breed of Silent Bird

Chaucer taught us we can make a jay
Say "Wat" as well as the pope, and Barnfield showed
That a deftly handled thorn will bring the cry
The nightingale sent back when gagging blood
Was all the tongue she had. The melody
That Yeats spun from his singing master's thread,
Now that he's but a gold and lacquered bird,
He sings all day to lady and to lord.

Well, I have trapped our jays, and since we host
No nightingales have tried our starlings as well
As several other birds that sing at roost
In nature. And I have fashioned many jewel-
Encrusted birds. The live have died, and rust
Has tarnished all my metal breed, but still
No single bird has sung a liquid note
For me or ever croaked a living "Wat."

Pastoral

The snow no longer holds,
The yellow-green unfolds,
The lecherous starling scolds;
    Therefore
Don't hold against the thaw,
Don't fold and kneel with awe,
Don't scold and chasten law,
    Ah! Lady, sweet Lady.

The sun has kissed the snow,
The leaves warm whispers blow,
The birds will never go;
    Therefore
Snow kisses on my face,
Blow sighs from my embrace,
Go softly to our loving place,
    Ah! Lady, golden Lady.

But snow will come again,
The russet leaves will rain,
The starling sing in pain;
     Therefore
Again refuse spring's thaw,
Rain, sleet, and thunder awe,
Pain chastens even law,
    Ah! Lady, bitter Lady.

Winter Pastoral

When the snow returns, the spring
Of brightest primrose fades;
When the trees are bare, no wing
The vanished green invades;
When the birds are gone, mutes bring
Their silent escapades.
  I knew all this
When we walked among old sheaves
Where yellow flowers grew,
When we lay beneath thick leaves
To talk of what we knew,
When the skies were loud with thieves
Who stole away the blue
  Ah! Fellow, wretched Man.

Martinmas Sermon

Text: Inasmuch as ye have done it unto one of the least
of these my brethren, ye have done it unto me.

A martin's upswung breast—O *chelidon*—
Cloaks in less than seconds the blue-black pass
We love, is driven from the fields and gone
For good when sparrows come—*domesticus.*

The things we love are fled too soon. The gay
And treble mouths of hounds, past clearing, brake,
And pond, we love an hour, two, a day.
Wild plum blooms, greybeard turns immaculate,

St. John's wort lingers on and summer dies
With showy gold; we love a week, a month,
A season. One face stops still our wandering eyes,
A breast the ache to touch, and thighs stop length

Of thighs. We love one year or five, or dozens.
But time mishandles bird and dog and bush.
Face, breast, and thighs he clutches, claws, and cozens,
St. Martin's cloak gone in a blue-black flash.

We have loved and had our coats dipped in blood,
Agonized and our garments parted, given
And the veils of our hearts pierced. But love withstood
Skies off the whistling dove and the soul unshriven.

26

There's Not Much to It

I will have lived for eighty years come fall,
Made crops for over half a century.
I've fathered fourteen children counting all
The Blacks, and yet I married holily.
Once I had a love as deep as sin,
And other loves that then, and now, I grieve.
No honorable man has held me in
Contempt; I keep no man in awe. I leave
A hoard of words that men will say my name
As long as men can read. But I must frown
When stopped and asked by all who'd play a game
With what appears to them a country clown—
And answer soberly each pleasant one:
"How goes it, Dad?"
                         "Why there's not much to it, Son."

In Your Beauty's Orient Deep

When I recall that corners of the stone
At Cheops were round before Herodotus
Had gazed with awe at days and works undone,
That beauty is old and time cannot efface
The lineaments of Eve, I realize
The Golden Fleece is Helen's hair, that all
Her wonder issued from the chrysalis
Of earlier glories.
               Twice-filled graves anele.
The bending neck as fragile as blown glass
That holds my modern lady's golden head
Is Nefretete's curving throat beneath
Egyptian mysteries and Giovanetta's
Pallid grace above the watered greed
Of Venice. The petal survives its fragrant death.

Noisome Weeds

Two years ago I placed a poem in
An academic magazine and urged,
Among other things, in a very thin
Voice, an elder gentleman, submerged

In critical and editorial gall,
To turn again to verse. But he was old
And listened to a young man not at all.
Besides the clatter was loud in roman bold.

And in a back room, daily, he would talk
To the local boys about the safest ways
To disc under unruly fumewort
Or other thick tares from careless days.

And in another place he would sometimes scold
At north county lads who had come to hear
About the sound husbandry of old
Tom Hardy's east forty, about Auden's gear.

But today I heard a rustle out among
The white page; the old man, sniffing rain,
Was putting in his seed where burrs had sprung.
He cried, "Master's in the garden again!"

Central Figure

—Santa Maria del Fiore

In Santa Maria del Fiore, an otiose
Restorer soils the reliquary rim
That holds the dust of St. Zenobius.
His trade is touching up the gesso gleam
Of another's or masking with a faceless lime
The stubborn scores of frescoes, mostly dross,
Now gone to dust with St. Zenobius.

Within a vast and awesome circling zone,
This wingless creature clings center to a choir
Of burning angels, spangled now in stone
Eternity. Upon his right, once fire
Played where Dante sat upon a chair
To watch this marble mount to triune glory,
Unmeasured miles apart from Purgatory.

Behind his back, Ghiberti (on whose urn
He drops cement) hung up the golden doors
Of Paradise. And on the left half-turn
A still unfinished piety abhors
With Michelangelo's stone eyes dull boors'
Unholy admiration looking up.
Before his face stood Donatello's shop

Where, chiseled out of time, once stood
A shriveled Magdalene whom only God
But not a man would touch. And overhead
The halo hangs that Brunelleschi wrought,
A virgin's vast and terrifying thought,
Ascending into heaven above this high
Hung man who plasters on eternity.

The Prince and the Tower

The golden shower is not the quickening god
Always, nor brings to man the hero winged
And querulous. The prince, amazed to find
That it could happen twice, —a tower ringed
With maiden hair—sees only a column blind
Against the sky, a shifting gold facade.
       Another tower, other gleams, the dark
       Hair of Rapunzel and the climb (the fall)
       Intrude. The field was then the same, the wall
       Of trees around, the distant singing lark.

All but the gold. Did he mistake the sun
Upon dark hair for promise and desire?
The tower, the tower, and now a face: two
Ladies and brightness out of the air conspire—
The spasm and the guilt—black kites pursue;
Sunlight warms the seed and shadows stun.
       Rapunzel, fled her cell, is standing near
       The prince. She does not see the destiny
       To which she moves; she looks behind, the cry
       Of the witch shrill in her uncovered ear.

The witch-cut hair released her from a cage:
The uncut hair had raised him to delight.
Before the violent severance, she urged
To go, he only to remain: her plight
To love, her plight to live high up then scourged
Them both, his blood warm, her tears of rage.
       The jagged ends are stained by blood from his
       Torn eyes not tears from hers. Rapunzel shrinks
       From tower, witch, and prince; the high-placed brinks
       Of passion still she flees as some abyss.

But passions stir him yet and still the height.
These second woven strands appear, and dull
Existence wanes; his voice begins to rise.
Rapunzel, turned away, hears the crying gull
In his song, would turn, but loathings tyrannize.
The prince rent once upon the thorns of spite
       Is torn again between the yielding briar
       And the rose: the rose seems now a yellow flame,
       The briar, though it falls away in shame,
       Has pierced his flesh and seared it once with fire.

Does the new fall of golden hair yield him
A way up or the lady a way down?
Is guilt an ebony staircase, desire
A yellow sunbeam? The rays fall upon dim
Landscape; ascent is lighted to the crown
But how can the prince make out the living fire
  From the reflected gleam? How tell the shadow from
  The man? Eyes in the tower see a new
  Creature and another girl to rue;
  Rapunzel looks back still; the witch goes dumb.

The Fourth Place

How wise you are not to contend or frown
Along with her who cried, "Not fourth nor loose
Like goslings following the gander and the goose
To some cold pond, where very like my down
Will not keep water out, and I might drown."

Why all the gaggling choir hear the word
And bathe in full beatitude: who spurns
One's swan capacity? The first place burns
With love; the second knows with pain; the third
Holds heavy throne. Singed, mad, and bent, each bird

Of these first three pays for the place it's in.
But fourth receives white wings before refined
In water and comes not near to sun nor mind
Nor weight before it feathers tender skin
With virtue or learns its power to bear its sin.

And Pays Us but with Age and Dust

Spring is late; the rains are old and gaunt;
The winters lengthen with our age, a jar
In the back-yard garden. Down the road a car
Spins its wheels in the mud. The time to plant
Rustles among the seed packets, and trays
In the garage spill soil from rotted corners.
The elder child leaves her crayon and strays
To the window to stare; she sees in the pane mourners
For birth; but the baby, too young last year,
Unaware of the door, turns at the mesh of a gear.

A Crown of Horn

I have a solitary unicorn
Who perished at the flood like all his kind;
But like a phoenix rose again, reborn,
And now he dies and rises without end.

O my high-leaping unicorn cavorts
To toss his head and fiercely thrust his horn.
His cry is heard in terrible reports,
While he harrows the valleys before me in scorn.

But that long horn has fabled properties:
It turns the poison meant for me to wine;
It saves me from the lion's savageries;
It sweats sweet water for my withering vine.

And O the horn is sharp and pricks me deep;
It brings bright blood to seep like any thorn.
And I will die upon that horn, then sleep,
Though lifted high upon that crown of unicorn.

The Thread

Once I left to wander down a maze
A tunnel cleft to hell, but me to harrow;
Then you held the thread knotted with days
Of love, and passion in a bed too narrow.

At other times I ran through seas on line
So light the gentlest drag had snapped me free.
But song was in your hands—the knots confine—
White siren notes from beds of ambergris.

The line was always there, spun from your womb,
But wrapped about my loins; pendant from you,
But me the spider hanging; slender as doom,
But proof against the intemperate winds that blew.

Now played, the line seems free; no catches pull
Me short. Yet now I tire; the rage is gone.
Wind up your threads, but watch the crying gull.
Wind up, wind up; the tides that flashed are wan.

A Remembrance of Some American Poets
(After Richard Barnfield)

Live Frost forever in your two-world dreams,
Whose love for this the other world redeems;
Old you may be, but your voice is young wisdom,
Prince of poets in an ancient kingdom.

And Eliot, serene eagle old in youth,
Whose wings loft wastelands to a mountain truth;
Out of the rocks of time, an aerie aloof,
You give to doubt's swift ages eternal proof.

And Tate, whose crisp Seasons render clear,
Spread double visions and surprise the ear;
Grow green your blasted landscapes, burning bush,
Violence of the soul in stately hush.

And Ransom you, whose gentle ironies rain
Verdure on a stippled, aching plain;
Write beauty again to soften the vehement line,
Those notes diminished, firm, restrained, benign.

    The sapling ages and the acorn dies,
    But leaf-imagined patterns stay the skies.

The Tower and the Maze

The prince was older now, and though he got
Rapunzel from the tower and lived with her
In the deep woods for several years, she cut
Her hair herself one day in remorse and fear.

The prince returned to court, his wife taking
Him back after much bitterness. Rapunzel
Married a commoner. The prince, seeking
Still golden stairs to a high stone sill,

Found a sleeping beauty in the attic but
Was caught by his black-haired princess just
As he kissed the girl awake. His wife had them put
In a maze of stout privet, where they were lost

Hopelessly for months. Not thigh by thigh
One night, they got separated; and though they heard
Each other's cries, they could not find the way
Back to each other's arms, each other's side.

Now lost from her and her, the prince about
And about went, lane on lane, for two years more,
Until in desperation he determined to cut
With his penknife straight through the hedge till clear.

His first penetration put him outside the maze.

The Historie of the World

Sir Walter received his visitor, a tall,
Austere but gently mannered nobleman
Who had a scratch upon his cheek of fine
And eloquent line. "My friend, you've had a cut.
I trust your foe bears not his hurt with ease."
Great Ralegh led his guest into the room
That legend caked with blood. Rich furniture
And tools of vigorous life could not dislodge
The ghosts inhabiting there of traitorous lords,
Adulterous queens and murdered kings, of those
Young princes, their muffled cries in measure to
The steps of Richard in the Abbey hall.
The host of living and the dead went on:
"But honor hides her head these days, as does
This king of timid grace, who puts his crown
Beneath his pillow night on night and calls
On God to fend off demons more from Spain
Than Tartarus and makes this once tall land
A nursery school for swaddling peace, while all
Those men of mine, of Drake's, of Grenville's, yes,
Those men of that now sleeping vanity,
That boy, that Essex, start the waters from
Beneath and roil this great Atlantic lake

42

That we were wont to call our sailing pond."
The proud man, frail now, hollow-cheeked, with blue
Tones mottling all his skin, went toward his desk
And leaned upon his hands, between which lay
A book of many pages, large, and faced
With boards and leather deep and darkly pressed
With characters. "That ugly ton of man,
Jonson, whom Wat, my son, so sorely plagued
In France, was here last summer—spoke the truth
In Commons—and wrote a verse or two to front
This volume of my *History* Burre has put
Up in his stalls. The duel that Ben fought
With that player made me think him just the man
To tutor Wat and keep the stallion's foot
From out too many nunnery doors. But that
Was back in ninety-eight, and he was marked
Upon the thumb with iron hotter than
The Queen's choice words. And now I hear they fined
A hangman just last week for branding of
A man, despite the iron's being cool."
Sir Walter's visitor began to speak
But courteously withheld his words the while
That restless energy pushed with some disdain
A manuscript beside the book and spoke
Again. "I saw a bit of violence in
The yard but yesterday. Some heated words
Were passed between a man in civil garb
And one in corselet and morion.
The unarmed man drew back his fist and struck

43

The officer upon the face. This man
Of steel (I take his heart to be a jelly)
Drew his sword and ran the helpless fool
Through skin and skin, who with his life's last blow,
In rare defiance, floored that coward soul.
Some of a throng who gathered at the spot
Took up the corpse while others bore the swine
Away. I doubt our James did slumber well
Last night to think that men can speak their anger
Out against the sword, or steel can pay
An insult out because one's honor's soiled."
The other man sat still through this report,
Yet indecision made the muscles play
About his mouth and jaws and several times
He seemed about to speak, but always his
Respect for that dark man controlled his tongue.
But when Sir Walter showed that he was through
By fingering once again the ordered sheaf
Beside the vellum of the folio,
The patient caller spoke. "You say you saw
This episode?" "From out the window there
Behind your head. I have so little room
Within this place to move myself that sound
Of any kind will draw me to that wall
And up upon that chest so I can pop
My head still out of doors and separate
It from my pent up body just as Coke
Would have me dressed upon the chopping block."
"Still pardon me, Sir Walter; let me ask

44

Again. You saw this fight?" "The fight? I told
You that I stood right there. But still, my friend,
Do you recall the tale about our judge—
I hear his enemies—Sir Francis in
The fore—are ready now to pull him from
The bench and stop his brawling voice in the land—
The tale they told when first he took our Bess—
My Bess, your Bess, everybody's Bess—
To bed? Sir William had been dead for a year;
And all our lads pursued my Lady Hatton
Either way: to take her for the night
Or for all nights if she would wed. She brought
With her a fortune even if a wasp's
Sting in her tongue was part the price. Sir Francis
Led the hunt, and Essex wrote to Burghley
On his Bacon's part, but from the yelping pack
This starveling Coke caught up the laggard hind.
He put his hand upon her belly when
They came to bed and felt a child to stir.
'What,' said he, 'flesh in the pot?' 'Yea,'
Quoth she, 'or else I'd never marry a Coke.'
Ha! she's led as many to Robin Hood's Bower
Since that night as ever she did before.
Perhaps Sir Francis Bacon among the rest.
Ha! Ha! I wonder if that potted flesh
Were pork." The caller smiled politely at
A jest he'd heard a score of times and now
Was fifteen years a relic. But then, he thought,
It's almost thirteen years that Ralegh's been

Confined, and Coke's vituperation at
The trial must rankle still. "But good Sir Walter,
Again I ask you if you closely watched
This courtyard brawl that in detail you tell
Me of. Forgive my urging you, but what
You say you saw, it cannot be. The man
In armor was a servant of the Count
Of Gondomar, your bitterest foe on earth,
And he it was who struck the blow. The man
Unarmed then wrenched the Spaniard's sword from his
Own sheath and ran the fellow through. And while
A stander-by knocked up the bloody sword,
Another Spaniard struck the murderer down:—
The dead man's comrades bore his body off."
Sir Walter spoke with smiles. At every word
He paced, gesticulated, pointed to
The casement, went to stand beside the square
Of light, and once looked out and down to see
The site he gazed on only yesterday.
"But good my friend, did not you hear? I saw
The bout; I took in every sound and stroke;
I cannot be mistaken. Your informant
Misconstrues. The Spaniard drew the sword;
The valiant man unarmored lost his life."
But as Sir Walter spoke the other shook
His head. "Dear, gentle knight, I may not but
With my disgrace deny your words, but I
Am he who wrestled with the Englishman,
And he who took away his sword, and he

46

Who haled him off to answer for this act,
And he who took, in holding him, this scratch
Upon my cheek." Sir Walter did not stop
His restless motions, not his pacing nor
His moving hands, but all his joy, so clear
Before, was faded out and something more
Than contradiction stirred an anger in
Him. The words he spoke were audible, but to
Himself more than his friend: "What is and what
Is not? I saw these things and give a true
Account, and you report the witness of
Your eyes, and we cannot agree. How can
I then reach truth when that I weigh the words
And deeds of kings and princes, statesmen dead
A thousand years and more. Why any man,
At any time, when he for current truth
Recounted faithfully confession of
His senses might have erred as I, and some
Romance upon which aftercomers pinned
Belief and cast their fortunes—nay, perhaps
On which some potentate entrusted crown
And state, subjects, reputation, and,
In cases I can contemplate, his soul—
Was nothing more than myth or fancy, dreams,
Hallucinations, or the misconstructions
Of the eyes and ears and what we reason with."
As his voice dropped, his passion rose. Enmeshed,
All faculties—that mind, those eyes, that strength—
Were bent upon the manuscript unfinished

47

On the ordered desk. He seized it with a cry,
And with a cry the caller leaped to keep
The pages from the fire; but Ralegh spun,
And with his back kept off the man until
A thousand pages, loosely spread about
The massive fireplace were consecrated
To the flames. With terrifying fury then
He turned and seized an onyx weight from off
The desk and whispered through his teeth: "Now do
Not be so rash and foolish that you spend
Your life on this so frail an enterprise.
I sacrifice these pages up to truth,
As I will you if you do interfere."
And as the caller settled slowly back,
And Ralegh rose in pride to his full height,
The fire brightly filled the terrible room.

GRAVE

A Sickbed Is a Grave

I think if any time before her third
Year, her frailty had faltered, stopped,
I would have missed her mightily and grieved
Some nights, and stared into the dark some weeks,
And pondered on this life, this death some years.
But now she's three and threatened; and because
I can't conceive her loss and can't refuse
Her plea, I will reject all forms of grief
And ask who's leaping into my child's grave.

Lady Ralegh's Lament
(1618)

Where is my garden now? And who my boughten
Assailant? What tree is this I'm speared so rude
Upon and do not die? I asked for water,
But they gave me gall. My garden stood
Not always on a skull. One tree that I was nailed
Against was good, though evil too; one spear,
Though sharp with pain, was my delight; full filled
With spear, I've died and died, but all the tears
I shed and water drank were sweet, no brow
With thorns to tangle in my hair. O Wat,
What garden have you sailed to now, and who
Its queen? And does it have a well? And might
I, if I found its current underground,
Swim through its water to my water pound?

Girod Street Cemetery: New Orleans

The dead here look upon the light from caves
Of the sun no longer tended; broken tombs
Of brick and mortar crumble into shallow graves,
And false spikenard bleeds crimson droplet dooms
That fall into the cracks from which they grow,

But rouse no passion in the stilted dust.
The walls about the crypts hold into breath
The living, and bright emerald lizards encrust
Grey stones that mount the sentinel to death.
The bones are white that never challenge snow.

Black happy children have their blind affairs
With laughter and discovery among
The rubble of their ancient games and cares:
Carruth, D'Aquin, Leroux—frail names once sung
Past time—are trod on in their overthrow

Or dispossessed from narrow beds of clay,
Preempted from the least they've ever known
By tired drunks who sleep as still as they
But do not suffer pillage of the stone,
Forever certain if forever slow.

Memento Mori

—Ash Wednesday

It is forty kilometers from Mantua
To Verona, and like long-dead Romeo
I plan to visit the tomb of Giulietta.

It is the fortieth ashen way I go
With faith. In every church in Christendom
The priest reminds us of our home below.

In every church in Italy we have come
Upon the skull in marble at the tomb
Of lover and saint, the face of martyrdom.

And we have come before to consider doom,
In verse that warns us all to fix love's end
Lest death surprise us in the lady's room.

To see love's end in the grave at Verona I spend
My way and finish out my fortieth year
On the sunlit road and take one final bend.

Around the bend the flesh is raped by fear,
With terrifying speed caught up and rushed
To exile by the grinning charioteer.

And though I'm caught by love, I deny it's lust.
I want no grinning skull. I want to know
How once I can forget I am but dust,
Escape awhile the grave's dry undertow.

The Patch-Nosed Snake

—Among other species, the young of the oviparous patch-
nosed snake cut their way out of their shells with an
"eggtooth," which they lose within a few days. They make
two excisions at right angles to each other.

Satan, there is no perfidy you keep as hell's:
I saw a son of yours or younger brother,
A roister-doister with jester stripes and false
Schnoz—a new-born patch-nosed snake—ralph
Into the world. He either knew I watched
Or thought to fool God himself, for as he hatched
His way out of a leathern egg (he gave himself
Away with that silly tooth-like chisel he fixed
On the end of his nose just for the purpose),
He made his opening in the sign of the cross;
And I swear I heard him hiss, "In the name of the Father
And of the Son and of the Holy Ghost."

The Shadow of the Blackbird

No Christ! Mercy made no hell like this!
Shot should have stopped the crows crying in my head,
Black birds that strangely stole the foliage
And left the nuts for my autumnal crop.
The birds cawed "fame," and with their wings they beat
My name so that it whirred and sang through the woods.
Yet only in my head the clatter rang.
But the leaden spreading column has only put
Me here. The birds perched in these branches are
No breed I've seen, but more articulate
Than crows they voice another's name,
Another's fame, another's fame, another's fame.
A second hell it is that this man's fame
Is built on graciousness to me (upon
My jealous soul the tunneling shrew repasts).
I do not know myself how much his early
Triumphs tautened my toe upon the trigger.
But hearing now those grieving lines for me,
That brass and marble utterance for me,
An elegy upon his friend, on me,
Beloved friend, that gives him fame and me—
Too much, you jealous God, you punish me
With everlasting acid shame to me.

Cold Maids

"For bonny sweet Robin is all my joy,'
Sweet Robin, cock Robin, sweet cock, sweet toy.
Beneath the water no seed for my boy,
All waters burst and gone my joy."

"Did she die, did she kill, was she sane, was she mad?
The fair, the rose, the maiden May self-dead?
Or did the rod, the branch although forbade
Knife deep with tears that covered her head?"

"She was fair, she is dead, she is gone without love,
Love you would say is the word of the dove.
She lies below with no man above.
Don't usher in death and tell me of love."

"Love's open wound, open womb beds the clown;
Love is the laugh puts the jester death down."

Toys of Desperation

This is a true saying and worthy of all
Men to be received: In the Lord's year
Nineteen sixty-six, I came into
The place of our God and the Madonna, Holy
Of Holies, tabernacle of flaming candles,
Santa Maria del Fiore. The ghost
Seemed great within me, and I climbed the stone
Tunnel that rises vertically to the dome.
Above, I stood on a balcony that rimmed
The turned-down cup and looked for the table below.
The devil, I say the devil (admit no metaphor
Here), the devil seized my waist to throw
Me from the cup to the tombs below. You hear?
That Satan Diabolo came into the world
    To have sinners.

I Am Black, but Comely, O Ye Daughters of Jerusalem

This year all the oaks but one in the great
Oak maze, the circle grove at Southwood, sough
A hundred years. They ring (dying in dim
Haphazard symmetry), twisted aslant
By their century of knotted growth, an oak,
Twice as large again around and more,
Whose date no one has reckoned. Mortared bricks
Veneered with cement seal its hollow trunk,
An empty core that does not leave enough
Seemingly of living wall to stead
So vast a skyward reach of limbs and leaves
And seed. Old Merc Johnson, planted, he says,
Six, seven years after the younger oaks,
Black, bent, knobbed, and rent like them, asks each time
We meet now, "Is de moanin' tree done split
As yit? Dis is de yar," he says; "Dis yar
She comin' out."

                                He tells a story of
A colored girl who, before his own birth,
Carried Captain John's child but ran away,
Into the palmetto hammocks with
A field nigger one day in her sixth month.
60

The night of her labor she struggled out of the glades
To have the child, to leave the child that she
Already loved on the Captain's land. She crawled
Into the riven oak, the only tree
Then on the lawn and almost half a mile
Below the house that stood atop the green
And gently rolling hill, the first cleared land
At Southwood. Even then the hole was big
Enough to hold her, swallow her in what Merc
Calls "her sepulchre and host, de wood
And iron of her upright coffin, de tomb
Of her flesh and de valley of her judgment, de gown
Of her shame and monument of piety,
De garden home of her sal-va-she-un."
She birthed the child near dawn in what must have been
Agony; for she passed out and was
Unconscious still when the Captain found her himself
At first light, walking in anguish but not alone,
Attended by a slave who said that when
He reached the tree, drawn by the crying child,
The Captain kissed the quiet girl. But what
Happened next Old Merc doesn't pretend
To understand; what he describes is the act
Of a man driven by visions of flesh that he loved
Yielded to another. The Captain had
Her chained and bricked up in the tree, at first
Intending the child to die with her, but he snatched
It out when several rows of brick had been laid.
The girl had recovered before the bricks were brought,

61

But was chained immobile in the trunk and had
Only her terror to stop her mind as she screamed
At the edge of human sound while the clay was bound
With mortar. After he pulled the child from the tree
The Captain sent a slave to Bonnet Pond,
Where cottonmouths were always in the sun,
To bring a fierce old fanger back, and when
The fearful black, who had poled a sluggish snake
Into a flour sack, returned with his load
Hung well out on the pole, the Captain, mad
And careless of the snake, emptied the
Resentful reptile in the hole, where from
The girl now came only bestial sounds.
Merc says folk tell the Captain screamed wild words:
"Was hell your garden? Satan your buck? Then here
He is again. Now take his kiss; now nurse
This child; now nest his fang." After the tree
Was closed, sounds continued for three days.
In that time the Captain had the slaves
Gather acorns from the oak and set
Them to bed. Merc says the tree made noises off
And on for years, but no one hereabouts,
Other than Merc, seems to go back to the time
They were heard. The spring beyond the tragedy
The acorns that had sprouted were carefully spaced
In nine concentric rings about the old
Live oak. The war ended that year, and Merc
Says now, "Dis is de yar; she comin' out."
I've played in and about that tree for near

To forty years. I remember clearly times
When the hole lay open. I remember too
Prying old bricks from the mossy ruins of
The great house, to be used to seal the oak
Again. The core was empty. No bones, no chains,
Nothing at all. But Merc is a notable liar.

As Yesterday When It Is Past
For Isaac Ash

That day we walked the row of sassafras
Between our fields, poor Isaac, you skirted brakes,
Tall weeds, and thickets, fearing hidden snakes.
A safer green, you thought, lay in the grass.

But grass is faded suddenly away;
Clover and phlox cut down like any flower;
All pastures shadow under the flying hour.
Firstfruit itself must fall upon mown hay.

     Abraham receive your son,
     A Lazarus too, his beggary done,
     Fraxinus nigra, now but dust,
     Sub *americana* thrust.
     Raise up, Lord, in serpentless lea,
     Redeem in ash the olive tree.